Houghton
Mifflin
Harcourt

CALIFORNIA JOURNEYS

Program Consultants

Shervaughnna Anderson · Marty Hougen

Carol Jago · Erik Palmer · Shane Templeton

Sheila Valencia · MaryEllen Vogt

Consulting Author · Irene Fountas

Printed in the U.S.A.

ISBN 978-0-54-454396-6

3 4 5 6 7 8 9 10 0918   23 22 21 20 19 18 17 16 15
4500568647   A B C D E F G

Unit 2

3

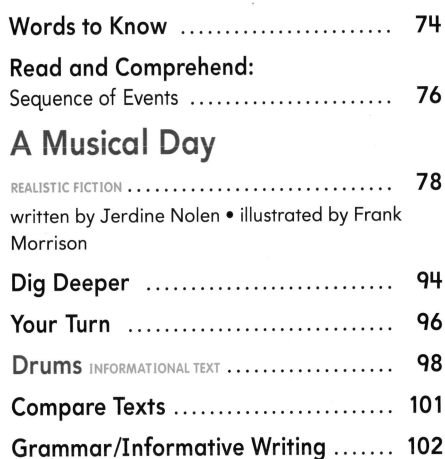

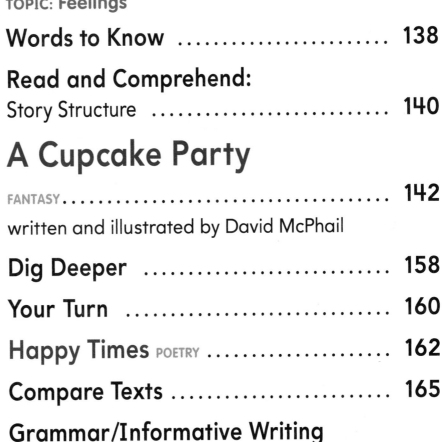

From Seed to Pumpkin

INFORMATIONAL TEXT

by Wendy Pfeffer • illustrated by
James Graham Hale

EXEMPLAR

Be a Reading Detective!

Welcome, Reader!

Your help is needed to find clues in texts. As a **Reading Detective**, you will need to **ask lots of questions.** You will also need to **read carefully.**

myNotebook

As you read, mark up the text. Save your work to **myNotebook**.

- Highlight details.
- Add notes and questions.
- Add new words to **myWordList.**

- Use letters and sounds you know to help you read the words.

- Look at the pictures.

- Think about what is happening.

Let's go!

Sharing Time

Stream to Start

Performance Task Preview

At the end of this unit, you will write a description of a character from a story you read. You will use details from the story to tell what the person is like.

hmhfyi.com

Channel One News®

9

🔍 LANGUAGE DETECTIVE

Talk About Words
Work with a partner. Choose one of the Context Cards. Add words to the sentence to tell more about the photo.

📓 myNotebook

Add new words to **myWordList**. Use them in your speaking and writing.

Words to Know

▶ Read each Context Card.

▶ Choose two blue words. Use them in sentences.

1 come

Wolf cubs come out of their den in the spring.

2 said

The ranger said that the cubs love to play.

 ELA RF.1.3g, SL.1.4, L.1.1j, L.1.6 ELD ELD.PI.1.6, ELD.PII.1.3a, ELD.PII.1.4, ELD.PII.1.5

3 call
A mother wolf can call to her cubs.

4 hear
Wolves hear better than people.

5 away
Wolves can travel far away from home.

6 every
Every wolf helps other wolves in its pack.

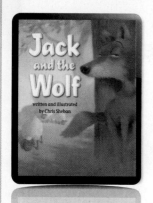

Read and Comprehend

☑ TARGET SKILL

Understanding Characters People and animals in a story are the **characters.** When you read, think about what the characters say and do. Use the text evidence to figure out what a character is like. Use a chart like this one to list text evidence about a character.

Words	Actions

☑ TARGET STRATEGY

Summarize Stop to tell about the main events as you read.

 ELA RL.1.3, RL.1.10a ELD ELD.PI.1.1, ELD.PI.1.3, ELD.PI.1.6, ELD.PI.1.12a

Traditional Stories

Fables are old stories.

They have been told for many years.

Fables can teach a lesson.

They can tell us how to act.

Jack and the Wolf is a fable.

It is about a boy who plays a trick.

Have you heard a story like this one?

Find out the lesson this story teaches.

💬 Talk About It

Which is your favorite old story? Why is it your favorite? Write answers to the questions. Share your ideas with your classmates.

ANCHOR TEXT

✓ **GENRE**

A **fable** is a short story that teaches a lesson. As you read, look for:

▶ a lesson about life
▶ events that happen over and over

Meet the Author and Illustrator

Chris Sheban

To create his artwork, Chris Sheban often uses watercolors and colored pencils. He has illustrated children's books and postage stamps. He joined with Tedd Arnold, Jerry Pinkney, and other artists to make the book **Why Did the Chicken Cross the Road?**

Jack and the Wolf

written and illustrated
by Chris Sheban

15

Once upon a time,
Jack sat on a big hill.

Jack had every sheep with him.
"It is not fun to sit," said Jack.

"I will yell **Wolf** for fun!"

His friends ran up the hill to help.
They did not see Wolf.

Jack sat back on the hill.
I will yell **Wolf**!

21

His friends ran back up the hill.
They did not see Wolf.

Jack sat back on the hill.

Wolf got up on a rock!

Jack and his sheep ran away.

"Did you hear me call?" said Jack.
"You did not come."

"You cannot trick us," said Nell.

"I will be good," said Jack.
"I will not trick you."

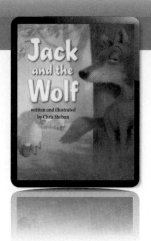

Dig Deeper

Use Clues to Analyze the Text

Learn more about Understanding Characters and Story Message. Then read **Jack and the Wolf** again.

Understanding Characters

Jack is a **character** in **Jack and the Wolf.** Think about what Jack says and does. You can use this text evidence to figure out what Jack is like. What does he do at the beginning of the story? What does he say? List text evidence about Jack and other characters in a chart to help you understand them better.

Words	Actions

ELA RL.1.2, RL.1.3 ELD ELD.PI.1.6, ELD.PI.1.7, ELD.PI.1.12a

Story Message

Jack and the Wolf is a fable. Most fables teach a lesson about how people should act.

In this story, one event happens more than once. What does Jack keep doing? What do his friends do? How does Jack change at the end of the story? This story has an important message. What lesson did you learn from it?

Your Turn

RETURN TO THE ESSENTIAL QUESTION

Turn and Talk

What lessons can you learn from story characters? Talk about the lesson Jack learns. Tell if you think he has changed the way he acts. Use text evidence to explain. Add your ideas to what your partner says.

💬 Classroom Conversation

Talk about these questions with your class.

1 Why does Jack yell **Wolf!** the first time?

2 What happens when Jack yells **Wolf!** the last time?

3 What lesson does Jack learn?

ELA RL.1.2, RL.1.7, SL.1.1b, L.1.1f ELD ELD.PI.1.3, ELD.PI.1.6, ELD.PI.1.7, ELD.PI.1.11, ELD.PI.1.12a

WRITE ABOUT READING ··································

Response Write words to tell what Jack is like. Look for text evidence. Use the words and pictures in the story to help you describe him.

Writing Tip

Add adjectives and other words to give more information about Jack.

☑ GENRE

A **fairy tale** is a story with characters that can do amazing things. These stories are very old and have been retold over many years.

☑ TEXT FOCUS

Fairy tales often have **storytelling phrases.** They begin with **once upon a time** and end with **happily ever after.** Find the phrases. What do they mean?

THE THREE LITTLE PIGS

Once upon a time, there were three little pigs.

The first pig made a straw house. Soon he could hear Wolf call out.

"Let me come in," said Wolf.

"No," said the pig.
"I'll huff and I'll puff. I'll blow
your house in," Wolf said.

The second pig made a stick house.
"Let me come in," said Wolf.
"No," said the pig.

"I'll huff and I'll puff. I'll blow your house in," Wolf said.

The third pig got bricks. He used every brick to make a strong house. Wolf could not blow this house in. Wolf gave up and ran away. The three pigs lived happily ever after.

Compare Texts

Read Together

TEXT TO TEXT

Compare Wolves Both stories have a wolf character. Tell how the wolves are alike and different. Use text evidence to fill in a chart.

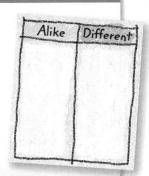

TEXT TO SELF

Write to Explain Think about the lesson Jack learns. Write about a time you made a mistake. Tell what you learned.

TEXT TO WORLD

Retell a Story Many stories use the words **once upon a time**. Retell **Jack and the Wolf** to a classmate. Begin with **once upon a time.**

ELA RL.1.2, RL.1.7, RL.1.9, L.1.6 **ELD** ELD.PI.1.6, ELD.PI.1.9, ELD.PI.1.12a

Grammar

Digital Resources

▶ Multimedia
Grammar Glossary

▶ GrammarSnap
Video

Read
Together

Complete Sentences A **sentence** is a group of words that tells a complete idea. It has two parts. The part that tells who or what is called the **subject.** The part that tells what someone or something does is called the **predicate.**

Subject	Predicate
Jan	sits on a hill.
Some sheep	eat.
One sheep	ran away.

ELA RF.1.1a, SL.1.6, L.1.1j ELD ELD.PI.1.1

Find three word groups that are sentences. Write them on a sheet of paper. Work with a partner. Take turns reading the subject and the predicate of each sentence. Then add words to make sentences from the other word groups.

1. Jack watches his sheep.

2. His dog helps him.

3. keeps the sheep safe

4. A wolf scares the sheep.

5. the sheep on the hill

Connect Grammar to Writing

When you proofread your writing, be sure each sentence tells a complete idea.

Informative Writing

✓ **Elaboration** When you write sentences that describe, use words that tell how things look, sound, smell, taste, and feel.

Ken wrote about a park to tell what it is like. Later, he added the word **smooth** to tell how the slide feels.

Revised Draft

smooth
The slide is fun.
  ∧

Writing Checklist

✓ **Elaboration** Did I use words that tell how my topic looks, sounds, smells, tastes, or feels?

✓ Did I spell my words correctly?

✓ Did I write complete sentences?

ELA W.1.2, L.1.1f, L.1.1j, L.1.2d ELD ELD.PI.1.10, ELD.PI.1.12a, ELD.PI.1.12b, ELD.PII.1.4, ELD.PII.1.5

In Ken's final copy, find words that tell how things in the park look, sound, smell, and feel. Then revise your writing. Use the Checklist.

Final Copy

The Park

The park has fields of green grass.

Tiny red flowers smell sweet.

The park has a playground, too.

The smooth slide is fun.

The silver swings are squeaky.

Talk About Words
Work with a partner.
Read the sentences on
the Context Cards.
Turn two of the
sentences into just one
sentence. Make sure
the new sentence is a
complete sentence.

Words to Know

▶ **Read each** Context Card.

▶ **Ask a question that uses
one of the blue words.**

---

① **of**

This bunch **of** flowers
smells sweet.

---

② **how**

How do cats see in the
dark?

3 make

She will make a loud sound in music class.

4 some

The boy sees some cows in the field.

5 why

Why do some people like a sour taste?

6 animal

This animal feels soft when the girl pets it.

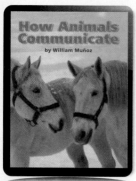

Read and Comprehend

☑ TARGET SKILL

Main Idea and Details Nonfiction selections are usually about one **topic**. They have a **main idea**, or one important idea, about the topic. **Details** are facts that tell more about the main idea. Details can give you a clearer idea of the topic. You can list the main idea and details about a topic in a web like this one.

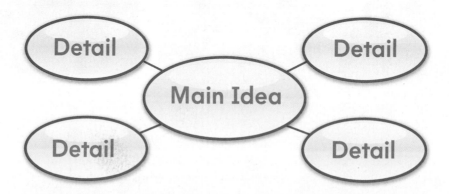

☑ TARGET STRATEGY

Infer/Predict Use text evidence to figure out ideas and what might happen next.

---

44 ELA RI.1.2, RI.1.10a, RI.1.10b, SL.1.4 ELD ELD.PI.1.1, ELD.PI.1.3, ELD.PI.1.5, ELD.PI.1.12a

Animal Communication

Animals can send messages.
Animals can understand messages.
Some move their bodies.
Many make special sounds.
Why do you think birds sing?
Why does a dog wag its tail?
You will learn all about animal messages in **How Animals Communicate.**

Talk About It

What do you know about animal messages? What would you like to know?

Share your ideas with your classmates. What did you learn from others?

ANCHOR TEXT

☑ **GENRE**

Informational text gives facts about a topic. Look for:

▸ information and facts in the words

▸ photos that show the real world

Meet the Author and Photographer

William Muñoz

From the mountains to the prairies, William Muñoz and his camera have traveled all over the United States. He has taken photos of alligators, bald eagles, bison, polar bears, and many other animals in their natural habitats.

How Animals Communicate

written with photographs by William Muñoz

ESSENTIAL QUESTION

How do animals communicate?

Animals Touch

An animal will tug and grab.

An animal can hug its baby.
How do elephants hug?

The dog and cat are friends.
How can you tell?

What is in the grass?
Animals can hear it.
They will run away from it.

A bird will sing—here I am!

A wolf will call to its pack—here I am!

Animals See

Why will a dog press its legs down?
It will let dogs see—I can play!

Some bees will buzz and dance if they find food.

Animals Smell

A mom can tell the smell of its baby.

An animal can have a bad smell.
It will make animals run away from it!

Touch

Hear

See

Smell

Tell what the mom can do.

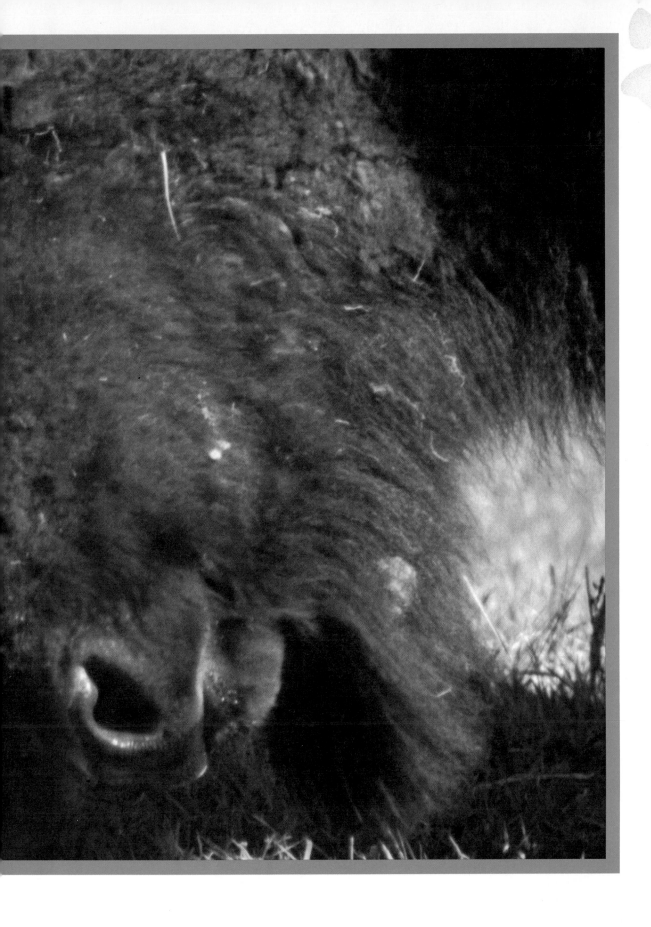

Dig Deeper

Read Together

Use Clues to Analyze the Text

Use these pages to learn about Main Idea and Details and Text and Graphic Features. Then read **How Animals Communicate** again.

Main Idea and Details

The **topic** is the one big idea that a selection is about. The **main idea** is the most important idea about the topic. Look back at the four parts of **How Animals Communicate**. What is the main idea? **Details** are facts about the main idea. What details do you learn? Use a web to show the main idea and details.

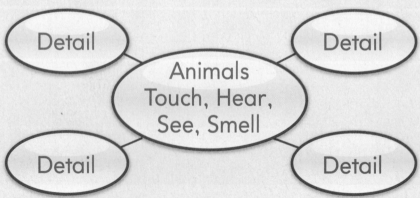

Text and Graphic Features

Authors use special words and pictures to tell more about a topic. A **heading** helps readers find information. It tells what a part of the selection is about.

Look back at the part called **Animals Hear**. What does the heading tell you about this part? What do you learn about the sounds animals make?

Animals Hear

Your Turn

RETURN TO THE ESSENTIAL QUESTION

Turn and Talk

How do animals communicate? Find text evidence to answer. Choose one of the senses that the author tells about. What details do you learn about that sense? Speak in complete sentences.

Classroom Conversation

Now talk about these questions with your class.

1 Why do animals send messages?

2 How do some animals show they like each other?

3 How are animal messages like people's messages?

ELA RI.1.2, RI.1.7, SL.1.6, L.1.1j ELD ELD.PI.1.6, ELD.PI.1.12a

WRITE ABOUT READING ··································

Response What is one fact you learned from the selection? Draw a picture to show the fact. Write a caption to tell about your picture.

Writing Tip

Add details to your caption to tell about your picture.

INFORMATIONAL TEXT

Insect Messages

Read Together

Insect Messages

An insect is an animal that has six legs. An insect's body has three parts. Most insects have wings so they can fly.

butterfly

Why do insects send messages? Some insects, such as mosquitoes, find each other by flying toward the sound that other mosquitoes' wings make. Honeybees can tell other honeybees where there is food. Every kind of insect has ways of sending messages.

honeybee

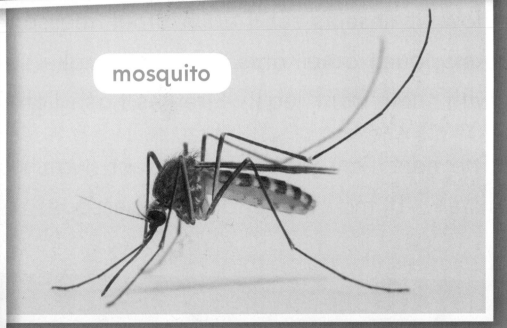

mosquito

ants

How do insects send each other messages?
Ants touch other ants. Crickets make sounds
with their front legs. Fireflies flash light.

The next time you see an insect, watch and
listen. It may be sending a message!

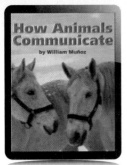

Compare Texts

Read Together

TEXT TO TEXT

Make a Chart Make a chart to tell what you learned about insects from each selection. Tell how the selections are alike and different.

TEXT TO SELF

Draw and Label Choose an animal you like from one of the selections to draw and label. Describe it to a partner.

TEXT TO WORLD

Discuss How do insects and other animals communicate? Use text evidence to explain. Why do animals and people communicate?

ELA RI.1.3, RI.1.9, SL.1.4 ELD ELD.PI.1.6, ELD.PI.1.12a

Grammar

Commas in a Series Commas are often used to separate a list of items in a sentence. A sentence with a list of three items will have a comma after each of the first two items. The word **and** is used before the last item.

Read Together

Our cats play, run, **and** jump.

He saw bears, elephants, **and** bees.

I like dogs, birds, **and** horses.

ELA L.1.1j, L.1.2c ELD ELD.PII.1.6, ELD.PII.1.7

Read the words on the line. On a sheet of paper, write each sentence using the underlined words. Use commas and the word **and** where they belong. Read your sentences with a partner.

1. Kittens like to <u>run   eat   play</u>.

2. I have <u>birds   mice   turtles</u>.

3. Horses eat <u>apples   carrots   hay</u>.

4. Bears can <u>tug   grab   hug</u>.

5. Bees will <u>buzz   dance   fly</u>.

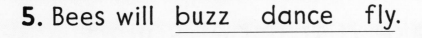

Connect Grammar to Writing

When you proofread your writing, be sure to use commas and the word **and** when you list three items in a sentence.

Informative Writing

✓ **Elaboration** A poem can describe a thing and give information about what it is like. It may also have words that rhyme.

Nori wrote a poem about elephants. Then she added details to paint a clearer picture for readers.

Revised Draft

long, gray

Elephants have ∧ trunks

that make a trumpet sound.

Writing Checklist

✓ **Elaboration** Did I choose clear words to describe or explain my topic?

✓ Did I use words that rhyme?

✓ Can I clap a rhythm to my poem?

ELA W.1.2, L.1.1f, L.1.1j **ELD** ELD.PI.1.10, ELD.PII.1.4, ELD.PII.1.5

Find details in Nori's poem that tell how things look, move, and sound. Then revise your writing. Use the Checklist.

Final Copy

Elephants

Elephants have
long, gray trunks
that make a trumpet sound.

They use their trunks
to eat and drink
and spray water all around.

A Musical Day
by Jerdine Nolen
illustrated by Frank Morrison

Drums

🔍 LANGUAGE DETECTIVE

Talk About Words
Work with a partner. Take turns asking and answering questions about the photos. Use the blue words in your questions and answers. Be sure your questions and answers are complete sentences.

ELA RF.1.3g, SL.1.1a, SL.1.2, SL.1.6, L.1.1j, L.1.6
ELD ELD.PI.1.1

Words to Know

Read Together

▶ Read each Context Card.

▶ Use a blue word to tell a story about a picture.

1 **our**
We like to play our games together.

2 **today**
The music class will practice today.

3 she

She likes to draw with her sister.

4 now

They eat lunch now.
Later they will play.

5 her

She took food for her lunch out of the bag.

6 would

Would you like to play with us?

Read and Comprehend

Read Together

✅ **TARGET SKILL**

Sequence of Events The events in a story are told in an order that makes sense. The **sequence of events** is what happens **first, next,** and **last.** Use a chart like this one to tell the order of story events.

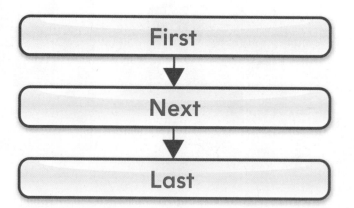

✅ **TARGET STRATEGY**

Analyze/Evaluate Tell what you think and how you feel about the story. Use text evidence to tell why.

ELA RL.1.3, RL.1.10a, SL.1.6, L.1.1j ELD ELD.PI.1.1, ELD.PI.1.3, ELD.PI.1.11, ELD.PI.1.12a, ELD.PII.1.2

Music

There are many ways to make music.

You can play instruments.

You can sing songs.

You may clap your hands to a beat.

Did you ever tap on a drum?

Did you ever blow a horn?

You will read about children making music in **A Musical Day.**

💬 Talk About It

What do you know about making music? Think about it. Complete the sentences. Talk about your ideas.

I know _____.

I would like to know more about _____.

ANCHOR TEXT

☑ **GENRE**

Realistic fiction is a story that could happen in real life. As you read, look for:

▶ characters who do things real people do

▶ events that could really happen

Meet the Author

Jerdine Nolen

Some kids collect baseball cards. Others collect shells. When Jerdine Nolen was a kid, she used to collect words. For a long time, **cucumber** was her favorite word. **Plantzilla** and **Raising Dragons** are two books Ms. Nolen has written.

Meet the Illustrator

Frank Morrison

Music and dance have always been part of Frank Morrison's life. He once toured the country as a dancer. The pictures he draws now are so lively they seem like they are dancing!

A Musical Day

written by Jerdine Nolen

illustrated by Frank Morrison

ESSENTIAL QUESTION

How is music part of
your everyday life?

Mom and Dad will go on a trip today.

Our Aunt Viv will be with us.
Tom and I are glad.

We get a big hug from Aunt Viv.
She is lots of fun!

We clap, hop, and sing.

Glen and Meg get here.
Now Aunt Viv has a plan.

She has a big bag.
A lot can fit in her bag.
What is in it?

"Would you kids like to play music?" Aunt Viv said.

"Yes!" we yell.

Meg and I make guitars to pluck.

Tom and Glen make drums to tap.

Tom, Glen, Meg, and I are a band.

It is fun to make music with Aunt Viv!

Dig Deeper

Read Together

Use Clues to Analyze the Text

Use these pages to learn more about Sequence of Events and Narrator. Then read **A Musical Day** again.

Sequence of Events

A Musical Day tells about what happens when Aunt Viv comes to visit. Think about the important events in the story. What happens **first, next,** and **last?** This order is called the **sequence of events.** Use a chart like this one to show the order of events in the story.

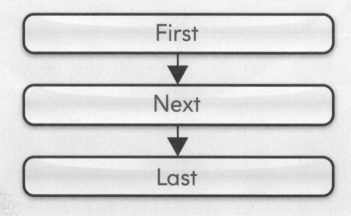

First

↓

Next

↓

Last

ELA RL.1.3, RL.1.6, RL.1.7 ELD ELD.PI.1.6, ELD.PI.1.7, ELD.PII.1.2

Narrator

Sometimes a character tells the story. This character is the **narrator.** The narrator may use words like **I,** **me,** and **my.**

Which character in **A Musical Day** tells the beginning of the story? How do you know? Look for text evidence in the words and pictures.

Who tells the story on pages 86–87? Who tells the rest of the story?

Your Turn

RETURN TO THE ESSENTIAL QUESTION

Turn and Talk

How is music part of your everyday life? How do the story characters feel about music? Tell the story to your partner like Aunt Viv would tell it. Use the pictures to help you tell what happens first, next, and last.

Classroom Conversation

Now talk about these questions with your class.

1 What happens at the beginning?

2 What do the children do after Aunt Viv gets there?

3 What did the children do that you also like to do? Why do you like it?

WRITE ABOUT READING ....

Response Why do you think the children like Aunt Viv? Write sentences to tell what you think. Give reasons why. Use text evidence such as words and details that tell what Aunt Viv is like.

Writing Tip

Add adjectives to help describe Aunt Viv.

INFORMATIONAL TEXT

Read Together

Drums

Informational text gives facts about a topic. It can be from a textbook, article, or website. Sometimes informational text can tell you how to do something. What does this article tell you how to do?

A **diagram** is a drawing that can show how something works. Find the diagram of a drum.

Drums

by Tim Pano

People around the world play drums. Yolanda Martinez plays drums. She makes drums, too. She sells her drums.

All drums have a frame. They have a drumhead, too. Drummers use a beater stick to play this drum.

Parts of a Drum

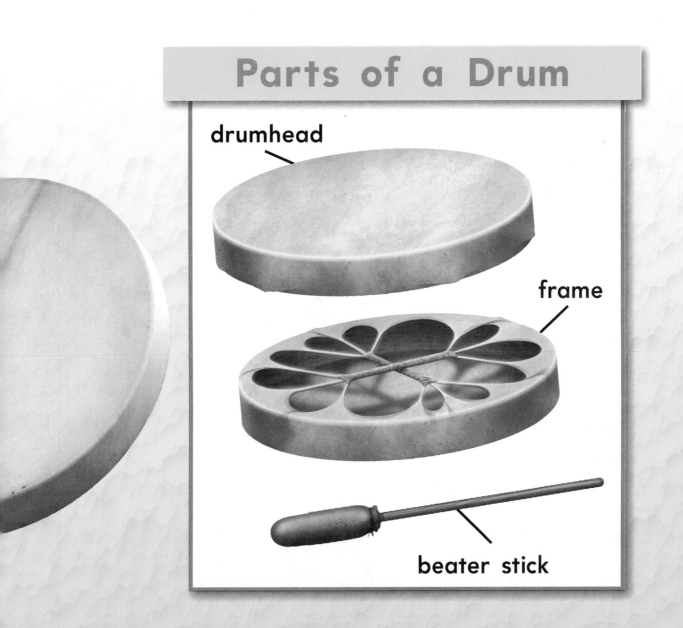

drumhead

frame

beater stick

Make a Drum

Would you like to make a drum today?
Try this.

1 Get an empty coffee can or
   an oatmeal carton.

2 Tape paper around the sides.

3 Now tape brown paper over the top.

We like to play
our drums.

Compare Texts

Read Together

TEXT TO TEXT

Making Music How do people in the stories share what they like to do? How do they make music? How do they make instruments? Share details.

TEXT TO SELF

Following Directions Tell the steps for making a drum. Have your partner repeat them. Then follow the steps to make a drum.

TEXT TO WORLD

Communication Think about what you learned in **Drums** and **Insect Messages**. Can drums be a way to communicate? Tell why or why not.

ELA RL.1.9, RI.1.9, SL.1.2a ELD ELD.PI.1.6, ELD.PI.1.12a

Grammar

Digital Resources

▶ Multimedia
Grammar Glossary

Statements A sentence that tells something is called a **statement**. A statement begins with a capital letter and ends with a period.

Read Together

The children like to make music.
They play for their class.
One girl taps a drum.

ELA RF.1.1a, L.1.1j

Find the three statements. Write them correctly on another sheet of paper.

1. my friends play in a band

2. sits at his drum set

3. she plucks a guitar

4. the very best singer

5. they have a lot of fun

Connect Grammar to Writing

When you proofread your writing, be sure each statement begins with a capital letter and ends with a period.

Informative Writing

Read Together

✅ **Purpose** You write a **thank-you note** to thank someone for something. Beth wrote a note. She changed words to make it clear that she is thanking her aunt. Beth also used exact adjectives like **soft** and **warm** to help tell why she is thankful.

Revised Draft

Thank you for
~~I like~~ the new hat. It is soft
^
and warm.

Writing Checklist

✅ **Purpose** Did I thank someone for something?

✅ Does my thank-you note have all five parts?

✅ Did I use capital letters, commas, and periods correctly?

ELA W.1.2, L.1.1f, L.1.2b ELD ELD.PI.1.10, ELD.PI.1.12b

Find sentences that tell what Beth is thankful for in her final copy. Find adjectives. Then revise your writing. Use the Checklist.

Final Copy

November 1, 2018

Dear Aunt Jess,

Thank you for the new hat. It is soft and warm. It has purple stripes just like my mittens.

Love,
Beth

Talk About Words
Verbs are words that
tell what people and
animals do. Work with
a partner. Find the
blue words that are
verbs. Take turns using
the words in complete
sentences.

Words to Know

Read Together

▶ **Read each Context Card.**

▶ **Use a blue word to tell about something you did.**

1 **write**

They write stories to read in class.

2 **read**

Dad will read a book to us.

3 pictures

He is looking for some pictures of lions.

4 draw

They all like to draw pictures.

5 was

This animal book was very funny!

6 after

They will go to sleep after the story.

Read and Comprehend

✓ TARGET SKILL

Text and Graphic Features Nonfiction selections use special features to point out information. These are things like **titles, labels, captions, photos, graphs,** or **artwork.** As you read, use special features to help you learn more about the topic. You can use a chart to list the features and what you learn.

Feature	Purpose

✓ TARGET STRATEGY

Question Ask questions about what you read. Look for text evidence to answer.

ELA RI.1.1, RI.1.5, RI.1.6, RI.1.7, RI.1.10a, SL.1.1a, SL.1.4, SL.1.5, SL.1.6, L.1.1j **ELD** ELD.PI.1.1, ELD.PI.1.3, ELD.PI.1.5, ELD.PI.1.11, ELD.PI.1.12a

Writing

Why do people write books?

They write to show how they feel.

They write to give information.

They write to make people laugh.

Authors can write stories, poems, and plays.

What do you like to write?

You will read about a famous writer in **Dr. Seuss.**

 Think | Draw | Pair | Share

What is your favorite book? Why? Think about it. Draw a picture. Tell a partner about it.

- ▸ Take turns speaking.
- ▸ Listen carefully.
- ▸ Use complete sentences.
- ▸ Use details.

ANCHOR TEXT

✓ GENRE

A **biography** tells about events in a real person's life. Look for:
▸ facts about why the person is important
▸ pictures of the person

Meet the Author

Helen Lester

Just like Dr. Seuss, Helen Lester has written a lot of books that make you laugh. She says that the funny characters she creates, such as Tacky the Penguin, are just like the students she had when she was a second-grade teacher.

Dr. Seuss

written by
Helen Lester

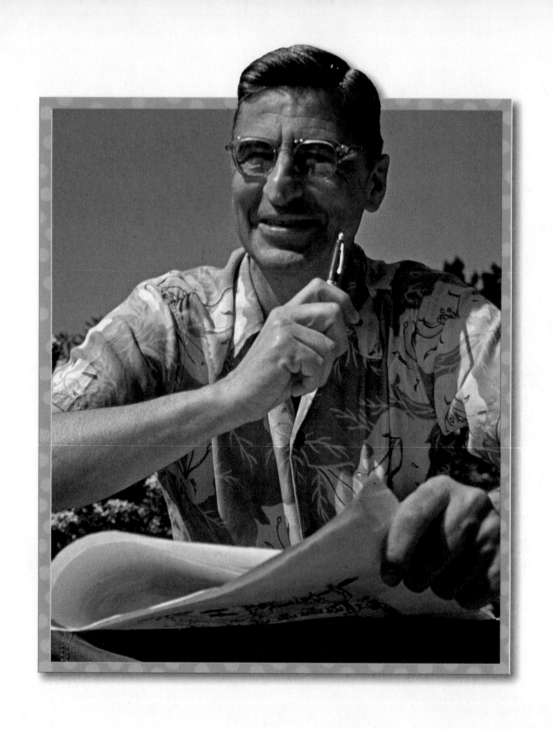

Here is Dr. Seuss.
You can call him Ted.
His mom and dad did!

Ted was a funny man.

Ted would draw pictures.

Here is a fun picture.

Ted would write, too.
Ted wrote the book
The Cat in the Hat.

The Cat in the Hat was a big hit!

Can you find the Cat in the Hat?

Ted had many big hits after
The Cat in the Hat.
Kids like **The Lorax** a lot.

Ted would write rhymes.
Can you find some here?

It was fun to hear Ted read.

Now kids can see animals
from his books.

Dr. Seuss National Memorial Sculpture Garden

Dr. Seuss is still a big
hit with kids today.

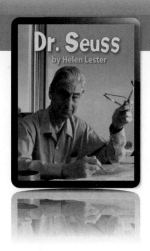

Dig Deeper

Use Clues to Analyze the Text

Use these pages to learn about Text and Graphic Features and Biographies. Then read **Dr. Seuss** again.

Text and Graphic Features

Dr. Seuss has special features that add information. **Photos** add to what the words say. What do you learn about Dr. Seuss from the photos? Why are some words in dark print? What do you learn about the Cat in the Hat from the words, photos, and artwork? Use a chart to list features and the information they show.

Feature	Purpose

Genre: Biography

Dr. Seuss is a **biography**. It tells true information about the life of Dr. Seuss. Look at the photos. They show the real man. What is he doing?

Look back at the selection for text evidence. Besides writing, what else did Dr. Seuss like to do? What other facts do you know about Dr. Seuss that could be in a biography?

Your Turn

RETURN TO THE ESSENTIAL QUESTION

Turn and Talk **What makes a story or poem funny?** Ask your partner questions about the animals Dr. Seuss made up. How do they make his stories funny? Look for text evidence to answer.

 Classroom Conversation

Now talk about these questions with your class.

1 What did Dr. Seuss write about and draw?

2 Why was Dr. Seuss an important person?

3 The selection says Dr. Seuss was funny. What pictures and words show this?

ELA RI.1.1, RI.1.7, RI.1.8, SL.1.2, L.1.1j ELD ELD.PI.1.5, ELD.PI.1.6, ELD.PI.1.7, ELD.PI.1.12a

WRITE ABOUT READING

Response Think about what you learned from the selection. What else do you want to know? Write questions you have about Dr. Seuss.

Writing Tip

Begin each question with a capital letter. End it with a question mark.

POETRY

Read Together

Let's Laugh!

GENRE

Poetry uses words in interesting ways to create feelings and describe things.

TEXT FOCUS

Rhyming words end the same way: <u>cat</u>, <u>hat</u>. **Alliteration** is a pattern of words with the same first sound: <u>big</u>, <u>bus</u>, <u>bed</u>. Find words like these that make the song and rhyme fun to read.

Let's Laugh!

Read this funny song with your class. Then sing it together. Use the same tune as **If You're Happy and You Know It.** Then sing it again with new rhyming words!

If You're Silly and You Know It

If you're silly and you know it,
say a rhyme — **fox, box!**

If you're silly and you know it,
say a rhyme — **red, sled!**

If you're silly and you know it,
then your face will surely show it.

If you're silly and you know it,
say a rhyme — **play, hooray!**

Peter Piper

Peter Piper picked a peck of pickled peppers.

A peck of pickled peppers Peter Piper picked.

If Peter Piper picked a peck of pickled peppers,

Where's the peck of pickled peppers

Peter Piper picked?

Mother Goose rhyme

Respond to Poetry

Pick the song or rhyme to memorize. Read and say it many times. Then, sing or say it for classmates. Use your voice to show your feelings.

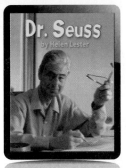

Compare Texts

Read Together

Express Opinions Look at the pictures in both selections. How are they alike and different? Which do you like best?

Connect to Language Arts Write a silly poem about your favorite animal. Use rhyming words and words that start with the same sound. Clap the rhythm.

cat
fat
pat

Describing Words Find words in the song that tell about things in the world. Which words tell how things look or sound or tell about feelings?

ELA RL.1.4, RI.1.9 ELD ELD.PI.1.6, ELD.PI.1.7, ELD.PI.1.8, ELD.PI.1.12a

Grammar

Singular and Plural Nouns Some nouns name **one**. Some nouns name **more than one**. An **s** ending means more than one. Some nouns change spelling to mean more than one.

(Read Together)

One	More Than One
hat	hat**s**

One	More Than One
man	men
woman	women
child	children

Choose the correct noun to name each picture.
Then take turns with a partner. Tell why you
chose a noun that names one or more than one.
Say a sentence using the word.

1. book   books

2. stamp   stamps

3. man   men

4. cat   cats

5. child   children

Connect Grammar to Writing

On a sheet of paper, write a sentence
with the correct noun for each picture.

Informative Writing

Read Together

✓ **Evidence** Before you start writing, plan the details for your **description**. A friend can help by asking you questions. Josh asked Evan about **The Cat in the Hat**.

Exploring a Topic

Does the cat have a tail? How do his feet look?

Prewriting Checklist

✓ Did I choose a topic I know a lot about?

✓ Do my details give information about how the character looks?

✓ Did I write adjectives to describe my topic?

Look for details in Evan's web. Then plan your own description. Use the Checklist.

Planning Web

Head
tall hat
red and white

Body
long, thin
tail

My Topic
Cat in the Hat

Arms
white gloves

Legs
two furry
feet

🔍 LANGUAGE DETECTIVE

Talk About Words
Work with a partner. Take turns using the blue words in complete sentences to tell about something you did. Ask questions if you are confused about what your partner said. Answer your partner's questions and explain things that are confusing.

Words to Know

Read
Together

▶ Read each Context Card.

▶ Choose two blue words. Use them in sentences.

1 **give**

She will give a gift to her friend.

2 **one**

There was one cupcake on the plate.

ELA RF.1.3g, SL.1.1c, SL.1.2, SL.1.3, SL.1.4, L.1.6
ELD ELD.PI.1.1, ELD.PI.1.5, ELD.PI.1.12a, ELD.PII.1.3a

3 small

The small red box is on the left.

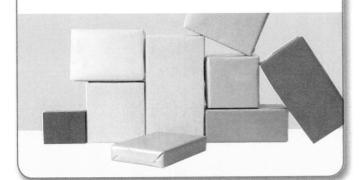

4 put

They put the party hats on their heads.

5 eat

The children eat pizza at the party.

6 take

They both take some balloons home.

Read and Comprehend

✅ TARGET SKILL

Story Structure A story has different parts. The **characters** are the people and animals. The **setting** is when and where a story takes place. The events make up the **plot.** The plot is often about a problem and how the characters solve it. You can use a story map to write text evidence about characters, setting, and plot.

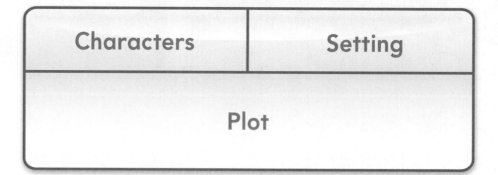

Characters	Setting
Plot	

✅ TARGET STRATEGY

Visualize To understand a story, picture in your mind what is happening as you read.

ELA RL.1.3, RL.1.7, RL.1.10a, SL.1.4, SL.1.6, L.1.1j **ELD** ELD.PI.1.1, ELD.PI.1.5, ELD.PI.1.6, ELD.PI.1.12a, ELD.PII.1.1

Feelings

Sometimes you feel happy.
Sometimes you may feel sad.
We have many different feelings.
You will read about friends and their
feelings in **A Cupcake Party.**

💬 **Think | Pair | Share**

How can you show your feelings?
Think about it. Complete the
sentences. Share your answers.

I feel ___ when I ___.

I show I'm ___ when I ___.

A Cupcake Party

written and illustrated by
David McPhail

A **fantasy** could not happen in real life. As you read, look for:
▸ animals who talk and act like people
▸ events that could not really happen

Meet the Author and Illustrator

David McPhail

David McPhail wanted to be a baseball player when he was growing up, but he wasn't good at sports. Next, Mr. McPhail wanted to play guitar in a band. Finally, he went to art school. He was great at drawing pictures and writing stories!

A Cupcake Party

written and illustrated by
David McPhail

ESSENTIAL QUESTION

How can you show a
friend that you care
about him or her?

"I miss my friends," Fritz said.
"I must have a big party!"

Fritz had a list of friends to
ask to his party.

Fritz went to ask Kit.
"I will come," Kit said.
"It will be grand!"

Fritz went to ask Jack next.

Jack said yes.

"A party is fun!" Jack said.

Fritz met Fran and Stan at a
tree stump.
Fran and Stan said yes, too.

Fritz went to ask Glen last.
"I will not miss it," Glen said.

Fritz baked cupcakes to
give to his friends.

He put a small picture
on every one.

Fritz felt glad to see his friends.

"Take the cupcake with a picture
of you on it," Fritz said.

His friends had a snack
for Fritz, too.

"Yum! Now we can eat
and have fun," Fritz said.

Dig Deeper

Read Together

Use Clues to Analyze the Text

Use these pages to learn about Story Structure and Dialogue. Then read **A Cupcake Party** again.

Story Structure

Fritz and Kit are two **characters** in **A Cupcake Party**. Who are the other characters in the story? Fritz's house is a **setting**. Where else does the story take place? The **plot** is the story events. What important events happen in the story? Use a story map to tell who is in the story, where they are, and what they do.

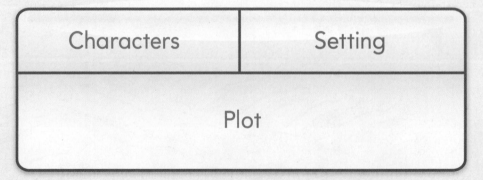

Characters	Setting
Plot	

ELA RL.1.3, RL.1.7 ELD ELD.PI.1.6, ELD.PI.1.7, ELD.PII.1.1

Dialogue

The words a character says are called **dialogue.** **Quotation marks** go around the words. The word **said** can show who is talking. Writers use dialogue to show what characters say, think, and feel.

What do the characters say when Fritz invites them to a party? As you read, think about who is talking and what the words would sound like out loud.

"A party is fun!"
Jack said.

Your Turn

RETURN TO THE ESSENTIAL QUESTION

 Turn and Talk

How can you show a friend that you care about him or her?

Describe the characters in the story. Tell how you know they are friends. How do you know this story is fantasy and not nonfiction?

💬💬 **Classroom Conversation**

Talk about these questions with your class.

1 What do the words the characters say tell you about them?

2 How does Fritz show that he cares about his friends?

3 Would you like to go to the party? Why?

ELA RL.1.5, RL.1.7, W.1.1, SL.1.4 ELD ELD.PI.1.3, ELD.PI.1.6, ELD.PI.1.7, ELD.PI.1.10, ELD.PI.1.11, ELD.PI.1.12a, ELD.PII.1.1, ELD.PII.1.2, ELD.PII.1.6

WRITE ABOUT READING ·······························

Response Write sentences to tell what you think Fritz is like. Give reasons why you think as you do. Use text evidence such as the words and pictures from the story for ideas.

Writing Tip

Use details from the story to help you think of good reasons for your opinion.

POETRY

Read Together

Happy Times

✓ **GENRE**

Poetry usually has shorter lines and words that rhyme. The words help show feelings.

✓ **TEXT FOCUS**

Rhythm is a pattern of beats in a poem. Sometimes it is easy to hear, like music. Some poems use a syllable pattern. This rhythm is not easy to hear. Which poems are easy to clap along with? Which poem is not?

Happy Times

What makes you glad?
What makes you sad?
Here are some poems
about how kids feel.

Singing-Time

I wake in the morning early
And always, the very first thing,
I poke out my head and I sit up in bed
And I sing and I sing and I sing.

by Rose Fyleman

I'm Glad

I'm glad the sky is painted blue.
And earth is painted green.
With such a lot of nice fresh air
All sandwiched in between.

Anonymous

Laughing Boy

In the falling snow
A laughing boy holds out his palms
Until they are white.

by Richard Wright

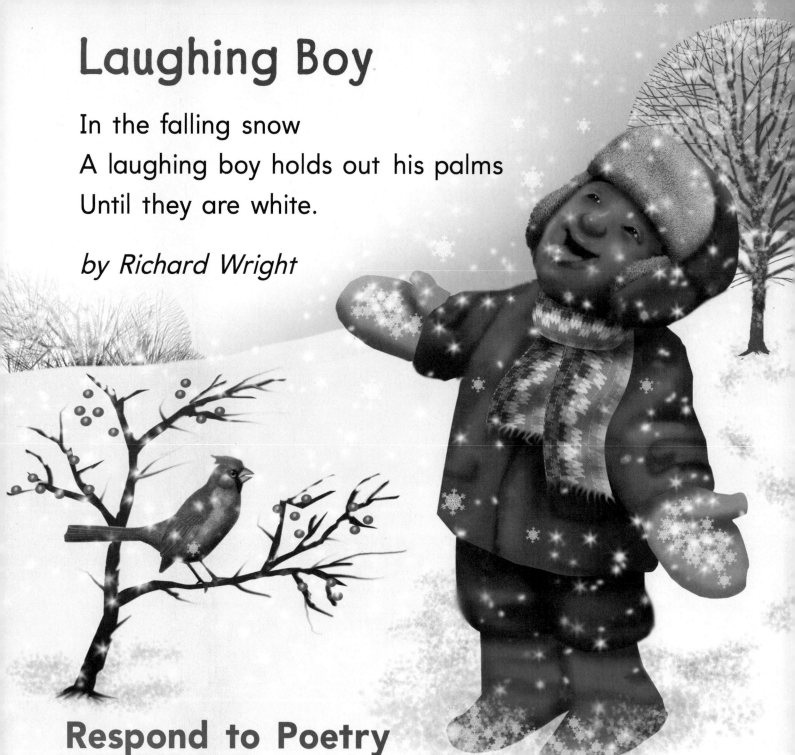

Respond to Poetry

- Listen to the poems again. Say what words or groups of words tell about feelings. Say more feeling words you know.

- Memorize a poem or rhyme. Say it for your classmates. Use your voice to show your feelings.

TEXT TO TEXT

Write About Feelings How do the characters show their feelings? Write words from the story and poems that tell how they feel.

TEXT TO SELF

Make a List Pretend you are having a party. Make a list of foods you would make for your guests.

TEXT TO WORLD

Write Sentences How do the characters in this unit help each other? Write sentences about how you can help a family member or neighbor.

ELA RL.1.4, RL.1.9 **ELD** ELD.PI.1.6, ELD.PI.1.7, ELD.PI.1.12a

Grammar

Digital Resources

▶ Multimedia
Grammar Glossary

Articles The words **a, an,** and **the** are special words called **articles.** Use **a** and **an** with nouns that name one. Use **a** before words that begin with a consonant sound. Use **an** before words that begin with a vowel sound. You can use **the** with nouns that name one <u>or</u> more than one.

Read Together

a **bear**

an **oven**

the **acorn**

the **cupcakes**

ELA L.1.1h ELD ELD.PII.1.4

Take turns reading the sentences with a partner. Decide which word belongs in each sentence. Write each sentence correctly on a sheet of paper.

1. I saw (a, an) chipmunk outside.

2. We sat by (an, the) tree.

3. They picked (an, the) plums for lunch.

4. Dad had (a, an) apple.

5. My friends ate (a, the) snacks.

Connect Grammar to Writing

When you revise your writing, be sure you use **a**, **an**, and **the** correctly with nouns.

Informative Writing

☑ **Organization** A good **description** begins with a topic sentence that tells what the description is about.

Evan wrote a draft of his description. Then he added a topic sentence.

Revised Draft

The cat looks very funny.
ᴧHis tall hat is red and white.

Revising Checklist

☑ Did I write a topic sentence?

☑ Did I give lots of information about how the character looks? Can I add adjectives?

☑ Did I use **a**, **an**, and **the** correctly?

Final Copy

The Cat in the Hat

The cat looks very funny.

His tall hat is red and white.

The cat wears white gloves.

He has a long, thin tail

and two furry feet.

He even wears a big, red

bow tie!

Write a Description

Read Together

TASK Look at **A Musical Day.** Who is having fun? Pick a boy or girl from the story whom you would like to describe. Then write a description to explain to classmates what this person is like.

PLAN ·

Gather Information Talk with a group about **A Musical Day.** What is each child doing? Find information in the text.

Now write ideas in your web.

- Who will you describe? This is your topic.

- What does the person look like? Describe the clothes, too.

- What does the person do?

- How does the person feel?

myNotebook

Use the tools in your eBook to remember facts about the character you picked.

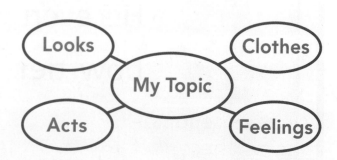

Looks · Clothes · My Topic · Acts · Feelings

ELA W.1.2, W.1.5, W.1.6, W.1.8, SL.1.4, L.1.1f, L.1.1g, L.1.1j, L.1.2c ELD ELD.PI.1.1, ELD.PI.1.10, ELD.PI.1.12a, ELD.PI.1.12b, ELD.PII.1.1, ELD.PII.1.3a, ELD.PII.1.4

DRAFT

Write a Description   Follow these steps.

Write your draft in *my*WriteSmart.

Topic Sentence

Will you write about Tom, Tom's sister, Glen, or Meg? Write a topic sentence to tell who you are writing about. Use one of these sentences or your own sentence.

_____ **is a** _____ **person.**

The word that describes _____ **is** _____ **.**

Facts

Write sentences to describe the person. Look at your web for ideas. Use adjectives and verbs to make your ideas clear. Use sentences like these or your own sentences.

_____ **likes to** _____ **,** _____ **, and** _____ **.**

_____ **wears** _____ **and** _____ **.**

_____ **feels** _____ **because** _____ **.**

Ending

Write an ending for your description. Use one of these ideas or your own idea.

- Tell why you like the person the best.
- Tell the most important thing to remember about the person.

Review Your Draft   Read your writing and make it better.   Use the Checklist.

✓WriteSmart

Ask a partner to read your draft. Talk about how you can make it better.

☑ Does my description describe a child from **A Musical Day?**

☑ Did I use information from the words and pictures in the story to write my facts?

☑ Did I use exact adjectives and verbs to describe the person clearly?

☑ Did I use commas correctly?

PRESENT

Share   Write or type a final copy of your description.   Add a picture. Pick a way to share.

- Read your description to a partner.

- Put it on a bulletin board.

Words to Know

Unit 2   High-Frequency Words

6 Jack and the Wolf
come
said
call
hear
away
every

7 How Animals Communicate
of
how
make
some
why
animal

8 A Musical Day
our
today
she
now
her
would

9 Dr. Seuss
write
read
pictures
draw
was
after

10 A Cupcake Party
give
one
small
put
eat
take

G1

A

aunt

Your **aunt** is the sister of your mother or your father.
I have one **aunt** on my father's side of the family.

B

baby

A **baby** is a very young child.
Tonya's family has a new
little **baby**.

baked

To **bake** is to cook in the oven.
My dad and I **baked** a cake for Mom's birthday.

band

A **band** is a group of people who play music together.
My brother plays drums in a **band**.

bees

A **bee** is an insect that can fly. The **bees** were buzzing around the flower.

bird

A **bird** is an animal with wings and feathers. Danny watched the **bird** fly away from the nest.

books

A **book** is a group of pages with words on them. We read **books** all the time at home.

C

cupcakes

A **cupcake** is a small, round cake. We ate **cupcakes** at Jenna's birthday party.

D

dance

To **dance** means to move your body to music. That song always makes me want to **dance**.

down

Down means going from a high place to a low place. She looked **down** from the top floor.

Dr.

Dr. is a short way to write **Doctor**. Our family goes to **Dr.** Lopez when we are sick.

E

elephants

An **elephant** is a very big animal with a long trunk. We saw five **elephants** at the zoo.

F

food
Food is what people or animals eat.
My favorite **food** is pasta.

G

guitars
A **guitar** is a musical
instrument. There are
two **guitars** in our band.

H

head
Your face and your ears are part of your **head**.
That man has a hat on his **head**.

hit
A **hit** is something that many people like.
That song was a **hit** with all the kids.

M

music
Music is sounds people make with instruments and their voices. My dad and I like to play folk **music**.

O

once upon a time
Once upon a time is a storytelling phrase that means long ago. Many stories begin with the words **once upon a time**.

P

party
A **party** is a time when people get together to have fun. I am going to have a **party** on my birthday.

R

rhymes
A **rhyme** is made up of words that have the same sound at the end. We say **rhymes** when we jump rope.

S

sheep

A **sheep** is an animal covered with wool. The **sheep** were eating grass on the hill.

smell

A **smell** is something that you sense with your nose. The skunk left a very strong **smell**.

T

tree

A **tree** is a kind of plant with branches and leaves. We have a big **tree** in our front yard.

trick

To **trick** is to get people to do something they do not want to do. She tried to **trick** us into giving her our lunch money.

W

wolf

A **wolf** is a wild animal that looks like a dog. The **wolf** watched the sheep very carefully.

wrote

Wrote means to write in the past. Tía Sofía **wrote** me a letter last week.

Acknowledgments

"Laughing Boy" from *Winter Poems* by Richard Wright. Copyright ©1973 by Richard Wright. Reprinted by permission of John Hawkins and Associates.

Credits

Placement Key:
(r) right, (l) left, (c) center, (t) top, (b) bottom, (bg) background